D1352386

KINGFISHER
Kingfisher Publications Plc
New Penderel House, 283-288 High Holborn, London WC1V 7HZ

First published in paperback by Kingfisher Publications Plc 1994
2 4 6 8 10 9 7 5 3 1
1BP/0500/SF/(FR)/135MA

Originally published in hardback under the series title Young World
This edition © copyright Kingfisher Publications Plc 2000
Text & Illustrations © copyright Kingfisher Publications Plc 1992

ISBN 1 85697 267 4

Phototypeset by Waveney Typesetters, Norwich
Printed in China

The Universe

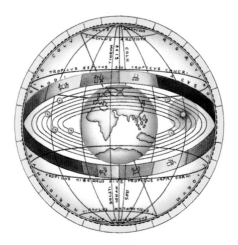

Kingfisher

Authors
Christopher Maynard and Jean-Pierre Verdet

Technical adviser
James Muirden

Series consultant
Brian Williams

Editor
Véronique Herbold

Designer
Christiane Beylier

Illustrators
Pierre Bon
Jean-Philippe Duponq
Luc Favreau
Gilbert Macé

About this book

For thousands of years people have looked up at the stars and wondered what lay beyond them.

Once people believed that the Earth was the centre of the Universe and that everything moved around it. Then they discovered that, in fact, the Earth moves around the Sun.

Today, powerful telescopes and space probes provide us with new, exciting information about the stars and planets, while rockets are able to send men and women into Space to explore. But even so, there is still much that we do not know about the Universe.

In this book you can find out about the Sun and the Moon and about the other planets that make up the Sun's family. You can discover how a star is born and learn about rockets and satellites. You will also find out about some of the still unsolved mysteries of the Universe.

CONTENTS

THE STARS

THE SOLAR SYSTEM

A JOURNEY INTO SPACE

DEEP IN SPACE

Studying

the
Universe

What is the Universe?

The Universe is everything that exists. The
Earth is part of the Universe. So are all the
other planets and the Moon and Sun.

Stars and clouds of gas and dust called
nebulae are also part of the Universe.
Scientists using telescopes and space probes
have learnt a great deal about the Universe.
But there is still much that we do not know.

Looking up at the sky

When we look up at the night sky (1), we can see hundreds of twinkling stars and a bright Moon. If we use a good pair of binoculars (2), we can see thousands more stars. We can also see that the surface of the Moon is covered with large craters.

1

2

A small telescope (3) will let us see smaller craters on the Moon and even more stars. With a giant telescope (4), scientists can see the Moon's surface in close-up. They can also see millions of stars far out in Space. But none of the stars look bigger than a dot of light, because they are so far away.

3

4

What is an observatory?

An observatory is a place where scientists called astronomers study the sky. It has giant telescopes that are kept inside big domes with sliding doors.

There are also cameras and computers that keep track of what the astronomers are looking at. Observatories are often built on mountains where the air is clear.

What is astronomy?

Astronomy is the study of the Universe.

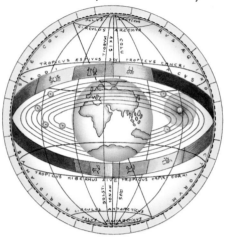

Early astronomers thought everything in the Universe circled around the Earth.

Later, a Polish astronomer called Copernicus suggested that, in fact, the Earth circles around the Sun.

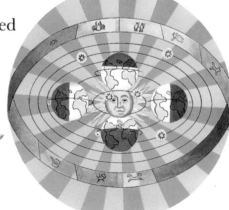

A scientist called Newton discovered what keeps the Earth moving steadily around the Sun. It is a force called gravity.

Today, astronomers believe that the Universe is getting bigger as huge groups of stars, called galaxies, move farther apart.

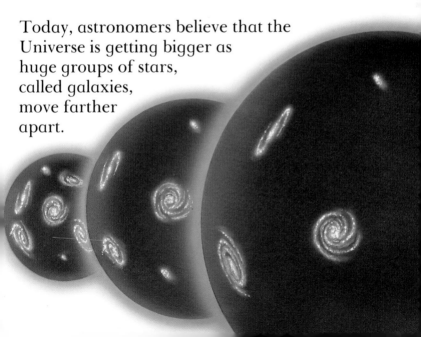

Amazing facts

Most astronomers believe that the Universe was born in a huge explosion called the 'Big Bang'. They think it took place between 15 and 20 billion years ago, long before the Sun and the Earth were formed. (A billion is 1,000 million)

Almost all stars are part of giant groups called galaxies. Astronomers think there might be as many as 100 billion galaxies in the Universe.

The Andromeda galaxy is the farthest object in Space that we can see without the help of binoculars or a telescope. This huge collection of stars is billions of kilometres farther away from the Earth than the Sun.

The Sun,

Earth and Moon

☀︎☾ Spinning in Space

Although we can't feel it, the Earth is always moving. It travels, or orbits, around the Sun. At the same time, the Moon is circling around the Earth. All the time, the Earth, Moon and Sun are also spinning round themselves.

The Earth takes one year to orbit the Sun.

The Moon travels once around the Earth every 29 days and 13 hours.

The Sun, Moon and Earth spin round on an imaginary line called an axis.

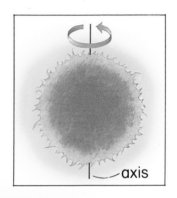

The Sun takes 27 days to spin round once on its axis. The Earth takes 24 hours.

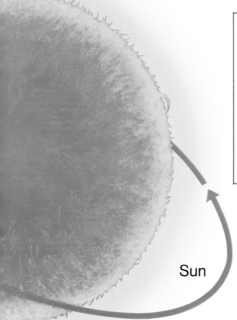

Sun

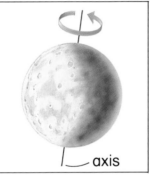

The Moon spins round once every 29 days and 13 hours.

☀️🌙 The Sun, our star

prominence

As the Sun rises, the night stars fade in its bright light.

The Sun is a star, the closest star to us in the Universe. Like all stars, it is a ball of hot, glowing gases.

Sometimes, jets of gas called prominences erupt from the Sun's surface. At other times, darker patches called sunspots appear. They look darker because they are much cooler than the rest of the Sun's surface.

sunspot

Remember: you must never look directly at the Sun, as it can damage your eyes.

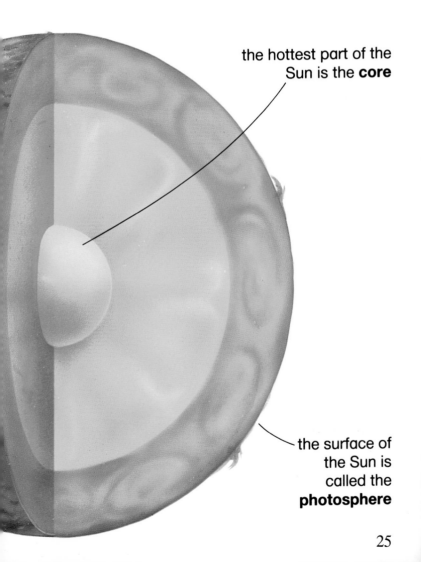

the hottest part of the Sun is the **core**

the surface of the Sun is called the **photosphere**

●) Studying the Sun

As the Moon circles the Earth, it sometimes comes between the Earth and the Sun. When this happens, the Sun is covered over. This is called an eclipse. During an eclipse, astronomers can study the plumes of glowing gas, called prominences, that rise up from the Sun's surface.

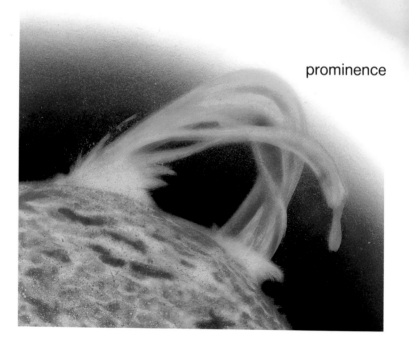

prominence

They can also study the cloud of gases that surrounds the Sun. This is called the corona. Although the gases in the corona are very hot, they shine a million times less brightly than the Sun's surface. This means they are usually invisible in full sunlight.

●) Day and night

The Earth is always spinning in Space. As it spins round, first one side of its surface is turned towards the Sun, then the other. This is why we have day and night.

When our side of the Earth is turned to the Sun's light, it is our day.

People on the dark side of the Earth are having night.

north

south

summer

winter

◐ The seasons

It takes a year for the Earth to travel once around the Sun. As it moves around, the seasons change. This is because the Earth's axis is tilted at an angle.

When the northern half of the Earth is tilted towards the Sun, it is summer there. But in the south it is winter. Six months later, the southern half of the Earth is tilted towards the Sun. So in the south it is summer, but in the north it is winter.

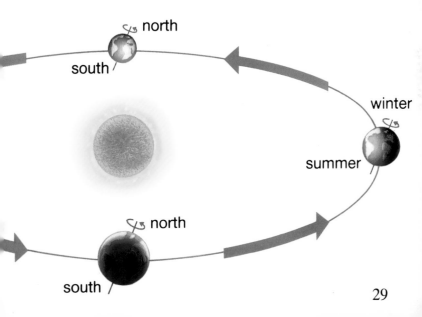

north

south

winter

summer

north

south

☀️🌙 Time zones

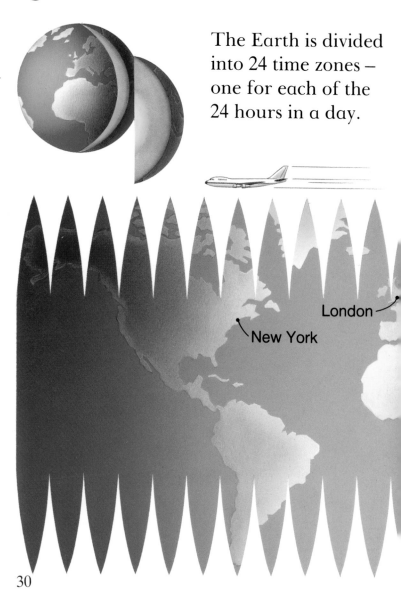

The Earth is divided into 24 time zones – one for each of the 24 hours in a day.

London

New York

Imagine the Earth as an orange cut into 24 slices, all laid out in a row. The clocks in each slice, or time zone, all show the same time. But the clocks in the next zone are different by one hour. So when it is 12 noon in London, it is 7a.m. in New York, because they are five time zones apart.

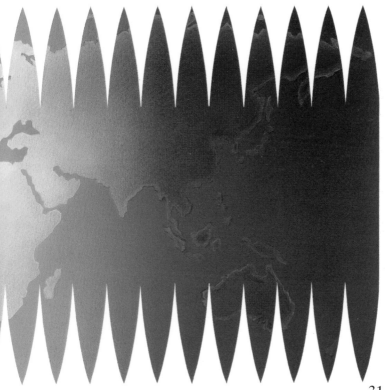

☽ The life-giving Sun

The Sun bathes the Earth with its light and warmth. Without it there would be no life on Earth. The Earth would be dark and far too cold for any living thing to survive.

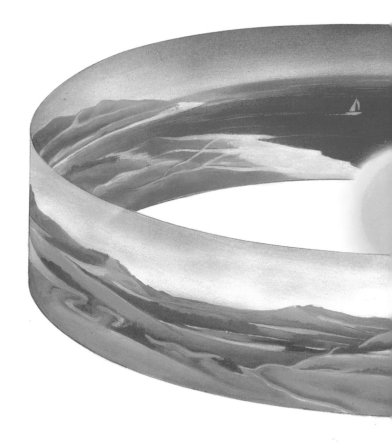

As well as light and warmth, plants and animals need water to survive. The Earth is the only planet we know of that has liquid water in seas, rivers and in the air.

●) Light and heat

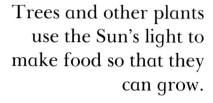

sunlight

Trees and other plants use the Sun's light to make food so that they can grow.

When plants make food, they also give out a gas called oxygen into the air. All animals and people must breathe oxygen in order to live. Without plants to make oxygen, none of us would be alive today.

plants give out
oxygen into the air

The Sun heats us and gives us light directly. But it can also be put to work to heat our homes and to make electricity. Solar panels trap heat from the Sun's rays and store it. It can then be used to heat our houses. Other kinds of solar panels use sunlight to create an electric current that can power the lights in our homes.

solar panels

●❱ Our nearest neighbour

Moon

Earth

The Moon is our nearest neighbour
in Space, but it is still about 380,000
kilometres away. Its surface is covered
with lots of craters and the sky above it
is always pitch black.

There is no air and no water on the Moon.
Without them, nothing can live there. The
craters were made when lumps of rock and
iron, called meteoroids, crashed into the
Moon's surface.

☀ ☽ The changing Moon

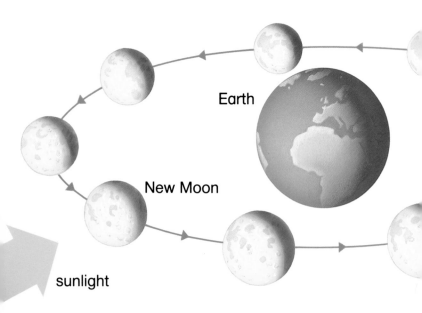

Earth

New Moon

sunlight

The Moon doesn't shine with its own light. We see it glowing in the sky because the light of the Sun shines on its surface. As the Moon travels around the Earth, all or part of it is lit up by the Sun. That is why, to us, the Moon seems to change shape.

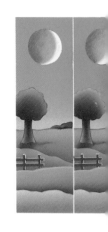

When the Moon lies between the Earth and the Sun, the side facing us is in darkness. We cannot see it at all. This is called a 'New Moon'. When the Moon is on the far side of the Earth from the Sun, we see all of one side lit up. We call this a 'Full Moon'.

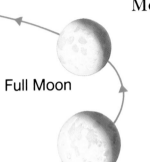

Full Moon

From Earth, the Moon may seem to change shape, but in fact, it is always round. The changes in its shape are called the phases of the Moon.

39

●) Moon and tides

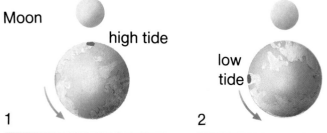

Moon

high tide

1

low
tide

2

high tide

low tide

Every day the oceans of the world rise and fall in a movement we call the tides. Tides are caused by the pull of the Moon on the Earth as they spin in Space. There are two high tides and two low tides every day.

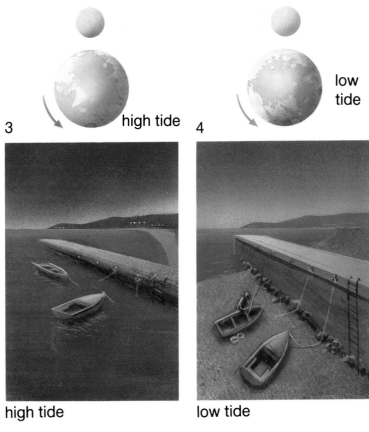

3 high tide 4 low tide

high tide   low tide

One high tide happens when the seashore is facing the Moon (1). The second happens when the Earth has moved around so that the seashore is opposite the Moon (3). In between there are low tides (2 and 4).

☀ ☽ What is an eclipse?

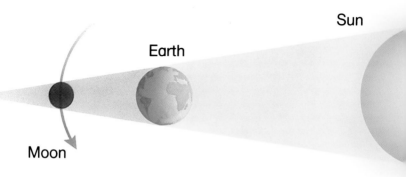

Sun

Earth

Moon

Sometimes, as the Earth orbits the Sun,
it comes between the Sun and the Moon.
When this happens, it throws a dark
shadow across the Moon. This is known as
an eclipse of the Moon, or a lunar eclipse.

42

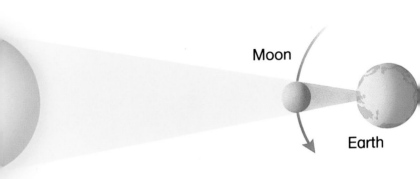

Moon

Earth

If the Moon comes between us and the Sun, it blocks out the Sun's light. The daytime sky darkens and for a few minutes the Sun appears to be blacked out. This is an eclipse of the Sun, or a solar eclipse.

Amazing facts

● ❭ The Sun burns up 240 million tonnes of fuel every minute. One day it will use up all this fuel and go cold, but scientists don't think this will happen for another five billion years.

● ❭ The temperature at the centre of the Sun is 15 million degrees Celsius. The surface temperature is much cooler – 5,500 degrees Celsius. This is still five times hotter than lava flowing out of a volcano.

● ❭ The Sun is about 150 million kilometres from the Earth. A jumbo jet would take 17 years to fly there.

● ❭ We only ever see one side of the Moon because it spins round on its axis in the same amount of time that it takes to orbit the Earth.

The stars

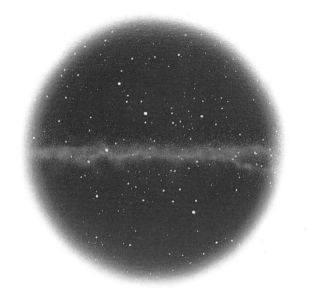

✸ Pictures in the sky

It is not easy to keep track of the thousands of stars in the sky. To make it easier, people since ancient times have grouped stars together. These groups are called constellations. Some are named after animals, others after ancient heroes or gods.

If you took an hour-long photo of the night sky, you would see that all the stars seem to spin slowly around one fixed point. In fact, it is really the Earth that is spinning. The fixed point in the northern skies is a star called Polaris, the Pole Star.

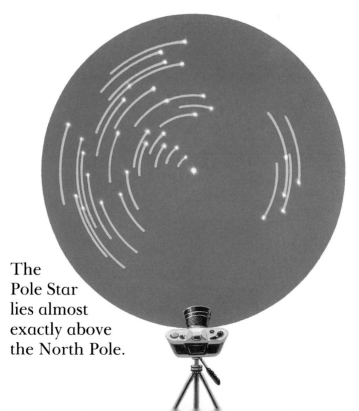

The Pole Star lies almost exactly above the North Pole.

✳ The constellations

There are 88 different constellations across the whole sky: the Great Bear, Orion the Hunter, the Scorpion, the Southern Cross, the Peacock and many others. But no one can see them all.

northern sky

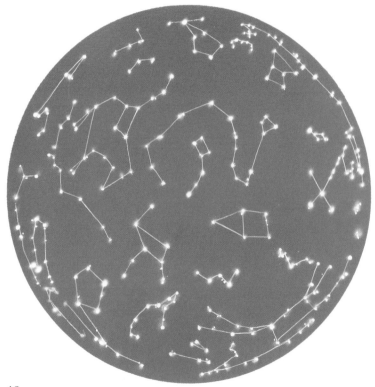

This is because people in the northern part of the world see different stars from people living in the south. There are far more bright stars in the southern skies than in the north.

southern sky

✹ The changing night sky

Month by month, as the Earth orbits the Sun, we can watch the constellations move across the sky. In summer, in northern skies, we can see the Little Bear with its long tail and the stars of the Dragon curling round it. To the left is the Great Bear. The group of stars shaped like a W is called Cassiopeia.

summer

In winter, a very different pattern of stars lies above you. Orion the Hunter, one of the most beautiful constellations, can now be clearly seen. The easiest part of Orion to pick out is the belt of three bright stars at his waist. Below Orion is a small group of stars called the Hare, while to the left is the constellation called the Great Dog.

winter

✳ Young and old stars

New stars are being born all the time in clouds of dust and gas called nebulae.

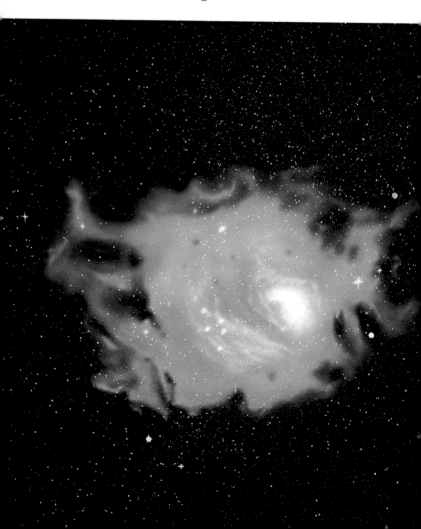

When you look up at the night sky, some of the stars you see are quite young. Others are middle-aged, like the Sun, and some are old and near the end of their life.

✸ The life of a star

A star is born when a cloud of gas and dust (1) shrinks into a ball (2). The ball gets hotter and hotter until it starts to glow as a newborn star. An average star shines for billions of years, burning up its gases (3). When it runs out of fuel, it swells up into a red giant (4). The red giant then starts to shrink (5 + 6) and becomes a white dwarf (7). The white dwarf slowly cools and fades to a cold black dwarf (8). Big stars turn into red supergiants (9). Instead of cooling down, they explode as supernovae (10) and for a short time burn more brightly than a billion Suns. What is left is either a neutron star (11) or, if the star was very big, a black hole (12).

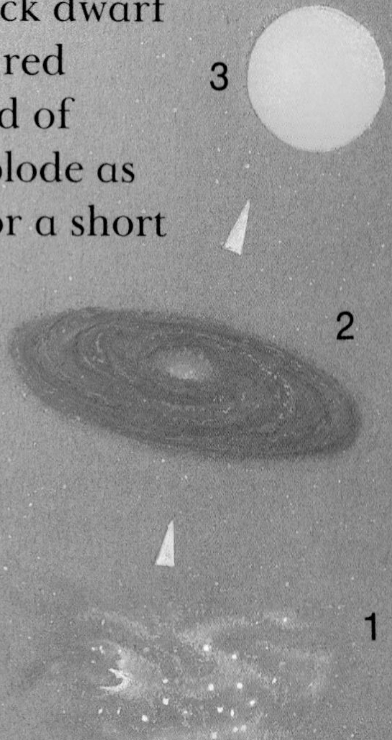

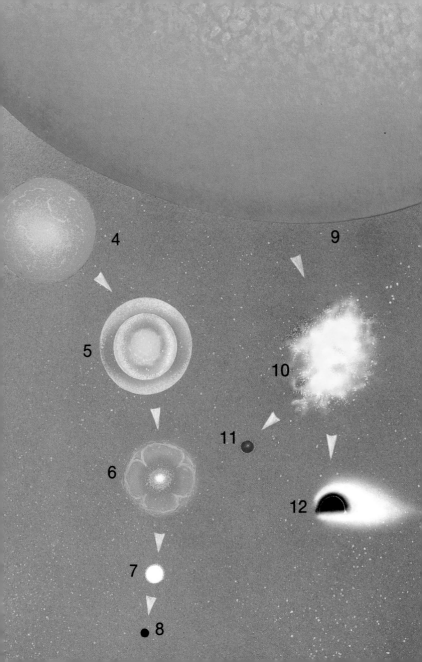

✸ The Milky Way

If you look up at the sky on a clear night, you will see a ribbon of white crossing it. In this ribbon, stars lie so close together they form a single band of light. You are looking at a small part of the Milky Way. The Milky Way is the name of our galaxy – the huge group of stars that is our home in Space.

This is what the Milky Way would look like from far out in Space. It is a great spiral of stars in the shape of a pinwheel. Our Sun lies two thirds of the way out from the centre of the galaxy. (In this picture the Sun is drawn bigger than it really is.)

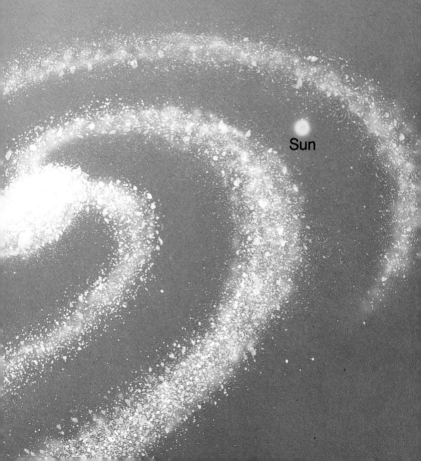

Sun

Amazing facts

Long ago, astronomers thought the Milky Way was made by gases escaping from the ground.

Stars have different colours. White and blue stars are the hottest. Yellow stars are cooler. Coolest of all are red stars.

Most stars shine steadily. But some brighten and then fade every few days, months or even years.

There could be up to 1,000 billion stars in the Milky Way. That's nearly 200 stars for every person living on the Earth.

The solar system

The Sun's family

The Sun's family is called the solar system.
It includes all the planets, moons, comets
and lumps of rock, dust and ice that orbit
the Sun. There are nine planets in the
solar system.

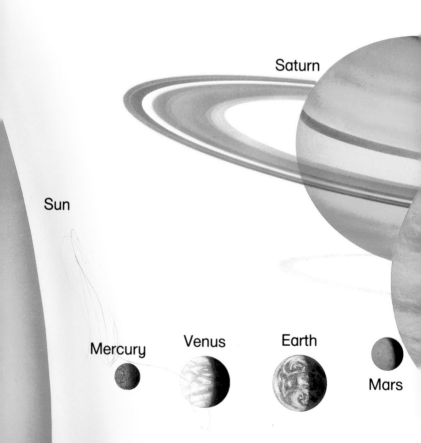

Saturn

Sun

Mercury

Venus

Earth

Mars

Neptune

Pluto

Uranus

Jupiter

61

Baking hot Mercury

Mercury is the closest planet to the Sun. It is a bare, rocky place not much larger than our Moon. Because it is so close to the Sun, Mercury only takes 88 Earth days to orbit the Sun.

Mercury

The space probe
Mariner 10 took the
first photographs of
Mercury's sun-baked
surface. It found a great
plain ringed by high
mountains.

There is no water or air on Mercury.
By day it is hotter than the hottest desert.
At night it is freezing cold. The ground is
covered with craters where chunks of rocks
from Space have crashed into it.

Stifling Venus

The second planet from the Sun is Venus. Venus is almost the same size as the Earth, but it is surrounded by thick clouds of hot, poisonous gases.

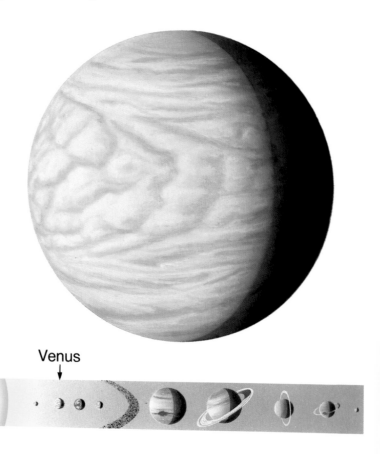

Venus

Several space probes have landed on Venus. They sent back information about the planet's surface, but were destroyed by the heat.

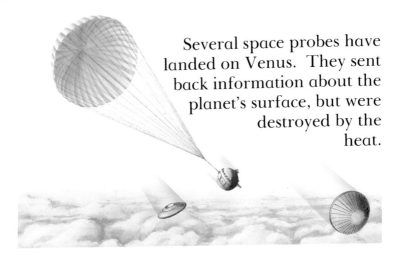

Venus is covered with volcanoes and old fields of lava. It is so hot that any water or liquid on the planet's surface dries up immediately.

The red planet

The rocks on Mars are full of rusted iron.
This is why the planet looks red. Huge
storms of dust can also make the sky
look pink.

Mars

Mars has two very odd little moons called Deimos and Phobos. They look like giant potatoes and are pitted with craters.

The space probe *Mariner 9* that orbited Mars discovered channels that look like dried-up river beds. But there is no liquid water on Mars now; it is all frozen in ice caps at the north and south poles. *Mariner 9* also discovered volcanoes on Mars. One of these, Olympus Mons, is the tallest mountain in the solar system.

Giant of the family

Jupiter is a huge ball of gases. It is the
biggest planet in the solar system. In 1979,
the space probe *Voyager 1* discovered a
ring of dust around
the planet.

Jupiter
↓

Jupiter has a huge red spot on its surface. Astronomers have puzzled over it for almost 400 years. We now know it is a giant storm three times bigger than the Earth.

Jupiter has 16 moons that spin around it. The four biggest ones are real giants; they are all bigger than the smallest planet, Pluto. These four moons were first spotted by the astronomer Galileo in 1610.

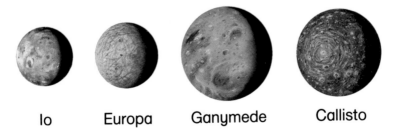

| Io | Europa | Ganymede | Callisto |

The ringed planet

Like Jupiter, Saturn is a giant ball of gases with a rocky core. From Earth it looks as if Saturn is surrounded by three wide rings. In fact, these rings are made up of thousands of narrow rings.

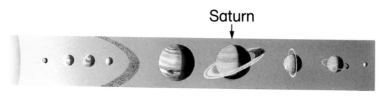

Saturn

Each of Saturn's rings is made up of dust and tiny bits of ice and rock.

Saturn has at least 18 moons, more than any other planet in the solar system. Titan, the biggest, is surrounded by a blanket of nitrogen gas.

Titan

Topsy-turvy planet

Uranus is the only planet
in the solar system to
orbit the Sun tipped
over on its side. It has
at least 11
narrow rings.

Uranus

Uranus takes about 84 Earth years to orbit the Sun. Its axis is tilted to one side so that its north or south pole sometimes points directly towards the Sun.

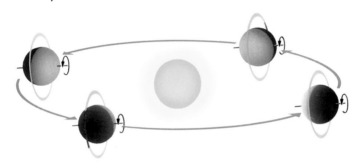

Uranus has 15 moons. Ten are so small that they were not discovered until *Voyager 2* flew past the planet in 1986. The five biggest are shown below.

Miranda

Ariel

Umbriel

Titania

Oberon

Stormy Neptune

Neptune is another gas giant. Some of the
fastest winds in the solar system blow
across its surface. The winds can reach
speeds of over 2,000
kilometres
an hour.

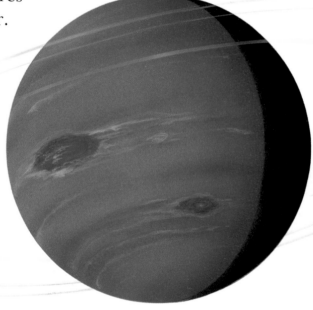

Neptune

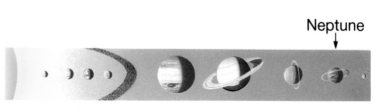

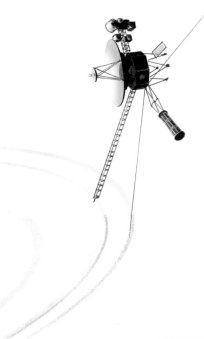

Voyager 2 visited Neptune in 1989. It discovered that the planet is surrounded by a set of rings. It also found streaks of white cloud around the planet.

Neptune has eight moons in all. But only two can be seen from Earth. The biggest moon, Triton, has a surface of ice that is split by giant cracks.

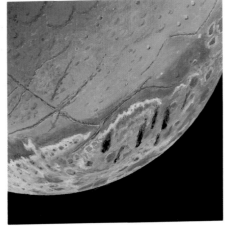

The last planet

Pluto is usually the most distant planet of all. But at the moment it is closer to the Sun than Neptune. No spacecraft has yet visited this small planet, so we know very little about it.

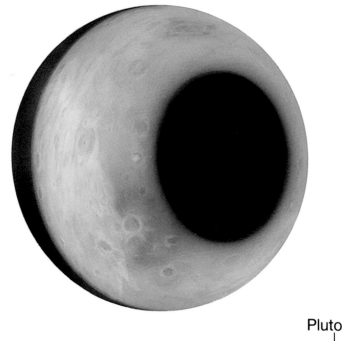

Pluto

Every 248 years, Pluto swings closer to the Sun than Neptune, because of its looping orbit.

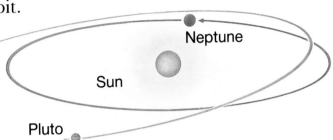

Neptune

Sun

Pluto

Charon

Pluto has one moon, Charon, that is half as big as itself. Charon is so close to Pluto that it often throws a huge shadow on to the planet's surface.

Astronomers wonder if there might not be a tenth planet even farther away from the Sun than Pluto. But so far, nothing has been found.

Meteors

Sometimes a brief trail of fire shoots across the night sky. This is a meteor. A meteor is caused by a grain of dust from Space. As it enters the blanket of gases that surrounds the Earth, the dust starts to burn up, leaving a glowing trail behind it.

There are also much bigger lumps of rock or iron called asteroids out in Space. Millions of asteroids orbit the Sun between Mars and Jupiter.

asteroids

The biggest asteroids are hundreds of kilometres wide, others are quite small. Sometimes a lump of rock that was once part of an asteroid collides with the Earth. This is called a meteorite.

In 1908, a meteorite 30 metres wide exploded above Siberia, knocking down trees 50 kilometres away. About 40,000 years ago, a huge meteorite carved out this great crater in Arizona, USA.

Fiery snowballs

tail

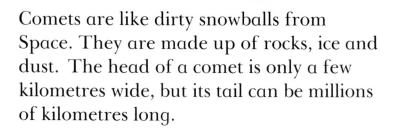

head of comet
made up of frozen
gases, ice and dust

Comets are like dirty snowballs from
Space. They are made up of rocks, ice and
dust. The head of a comet is only a few
kilometres wide, but its tail can be millions
of kilometres long.

Comets orbit the Sun in long, looping orbits. Most of the time we cannot see them. But when comets come close to the Sun, its heat turns their ice into gas. The gas and dust flow off into Space in a glowing tail that always points away from the Sun.

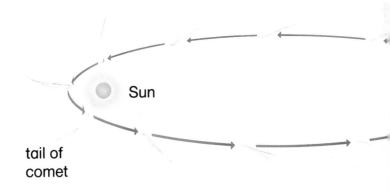

Sun

tail of comet

Amazing facts

All nine planets in the solar system, squashed together, would fit inside the Sun 600 times.

The temperature on the surface of Venus is hot enough to bake clay pottery.

Two mathematicians worked out that Neptune existed before it was actually discovered. They calculated where it was by the way its pull made Uranus slow down in its orbit.

Io, one of Jupiter's moons, has more active volcanoes than any other moon or planet in the solar system.

A journey

into Space

Going to the Moon

On 21 July, 1969 the American astronauts Neil Armstrong and Edwin Aldrin were the first people to land on the Moon. The two astronauts dug up pieces of rock and set up instruments that could measure moonquakes.

Between 1969 and 1972, five other crews of astronauts landed on the Moon. In 1971, the *Apollo 15* mission was the first to use the lunar buggy. The astronauts travelled about 30 kilometres in the buggy, exploring the Moon's surface.

☄ Space training

In Space nothing has any weight.
Astronauts have to
get used to being
as light as
a balloon.

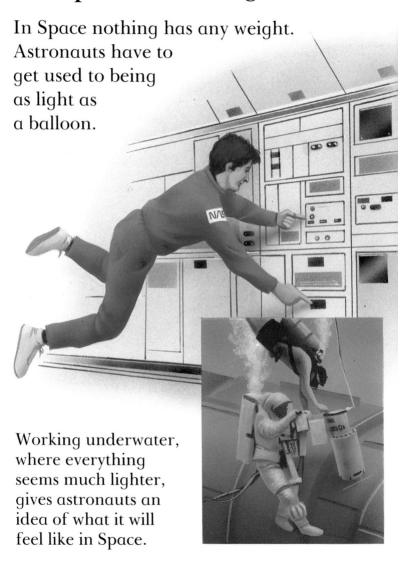

Working underwater,
where everything
seems much lighter,
gives astronauts an
idea of what it will
feel like in Space.

At lift-off, astronauts feel as if they are being crushed by a great weight. They prepare for this by training on a machine called a centrifuge that spins them round very fast.

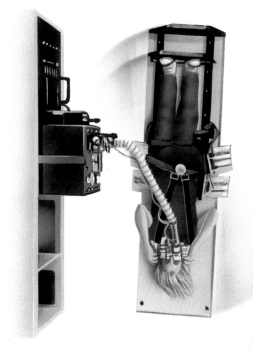

In Space there is no up or down. Astronauts train on revolving chairs to help them get used to working in any position, even upside-down.

◀▪◆ Working in Space

There is no air in Space, so astronauts must wear a spacesuit with its own air supply when they work outside their spacecraft.

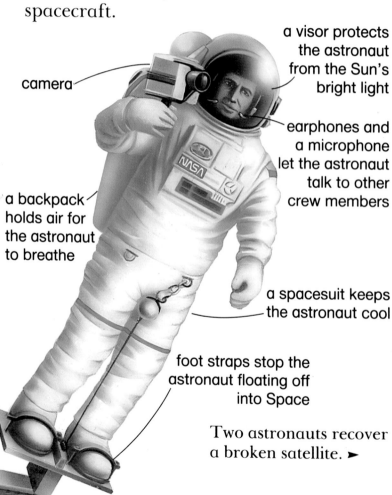

a visor protects the astronaut from the Sun's bright light

camera

earphones and a microphone let the astronaut talk to other crew members

a backpack holds air for the astronaut to breathe

a spacesuit keeps the astronaut cool

foot straps stop the astronaut floating off into Space

Two astronauts recover a broken satellite. ➤

Life in Space

Even everyday activities can be very different in Space.

Astronauts still have to exercise. But you couldn't pedal a bike like this on Earth!

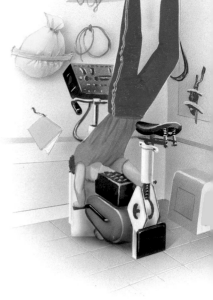

Sleeping upright is just as comfortable as lying down once you are in Space. But astronauts have to strap themselves into their sleeping bags so that they don't float away in their sleep.

Spacecraft are designed to make living in Space as comfortable as possible for the astronauts. This way, astronauts can stay out in Space for days, weeks or even months at a time.

Keeping clean in Space isn't easy. Some spacecraft have special showers for the astronauts. The water has to be sucked away, otherwise the water drops would float off.

◄═◄ Mission control

Every trip into Space is run from a mission control centre. Here, controllers keep track of the entire flight on their computer screens.

Mission control keeps in contact with the astronauts all the time. If there is a problem, they can even take control of the spacecraft.

Rockets

Rockets are used to carry things into Space. *Ariane 5* is a new rocket that will be able to lift several satellites and space probes into Space at once. *Ariane 5* is divided into two parts, or stages. The first stage is made up of a huge fuel tank and a powerful engine. There are also two booster rockets to give extra power at lift-off. The cargo, or payload, is carried in the second stage.

payload

ariane 5

esa

esa

cnes

cnes

booster rockets

94

Once their fuel has been used up, the booster rockets and the first stage separate and fall away.

4. All that is left of the huge rocket is its payload.

3. The first stage separates. It will burn up as it falls back to Earth.

2. The protective covering around the second stage comes away.

1. Soon after lift-off, the two booster rockets fall away and parachute into the sea.

⬤ The space shuttle

The space shuttle can lift off into Space
like a rocket and then come back to Earth
like a glider. It can carry a crew of up to
seven astronauts and can also carry loads
as big as a coach in its payload bay.

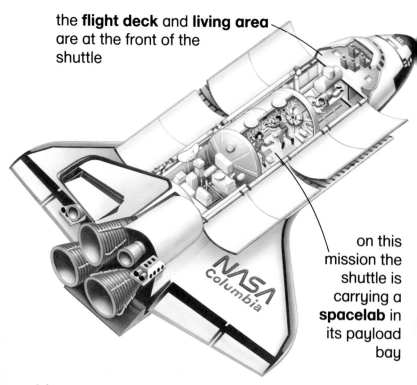

the **flight deck** and **living area**
are at the front of the
shuttle

on this
mission the
shuttle is
carrying a
spacelab in
its payload
bay

The shuttle is more powerful than 100 jumbo jets. It takes eight minutes to travel into Space. At the end of its mission, it lands like a glider. Unlike other rockets, the shuttle can be used again.

Satellites

Hundreds of satellites have been put into orbit around the Earth by rockets. Some bring us television pictures from the other side of the world. Others are used by ships or planes to help them navigate.

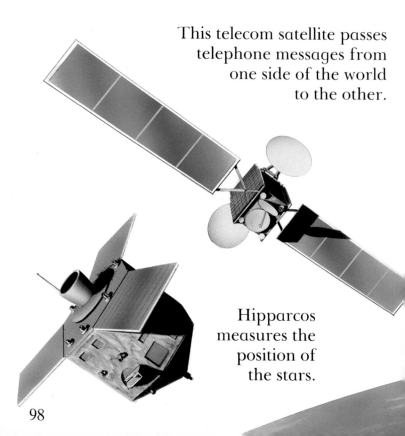

This telecom satellite passes telephone messages from one side of the world to the other.

Hipparcos measures the position of the stars.

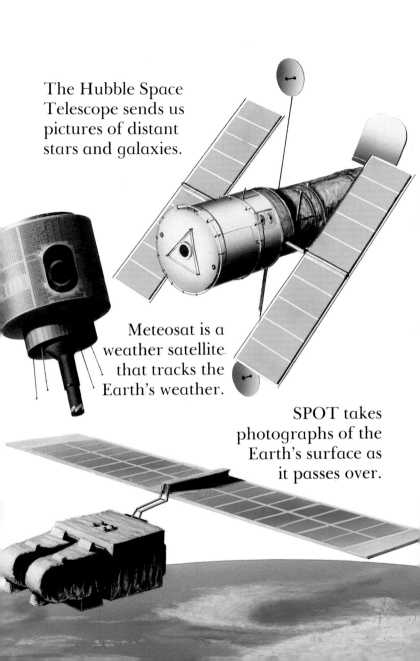

The Hubble Space Telescope sends us pictures of distant stars and galaxies.

Meteosat is a weather satellite that tracks the Earth's weather.

SPOT takes photographs of the Earth's surface as it passes over.

Space probes

Unmanned space probes are sent on long journeys into Space without any chance of ever returning to Earth. Most are used to study the other planets in our solar system. One of the most famous probes, *Voyager 2*, has already visited Jupiter, Saturn, Uranus and Neptune.

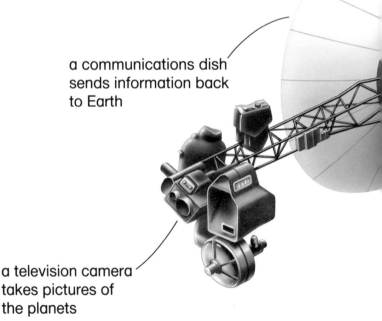

a communications dish sends information back to Earth

a television camera takes pictures of the planets

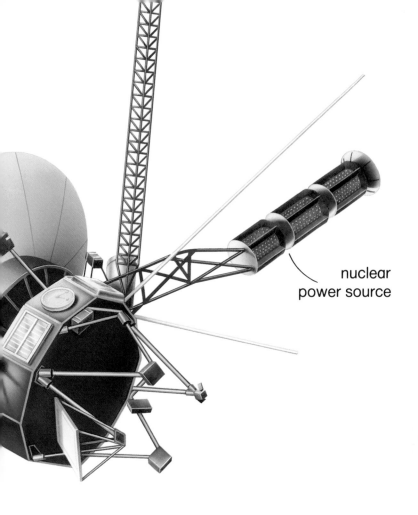

nuclear
power source

Voyager 2 is now
leaving our solar
system and heading
out into Deep Space.

Space station

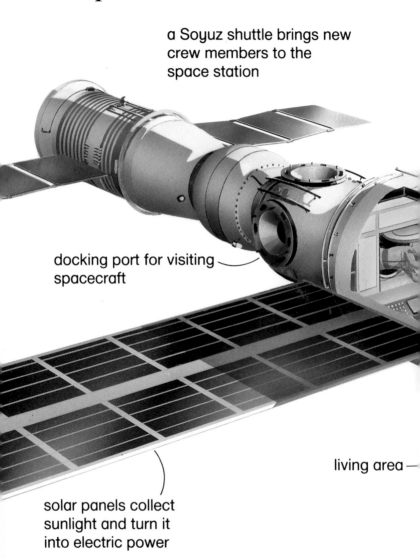

a Soyuz shuttle brings new crew members to the space station

docking port for visiting spacecraft

living area—

solar panels collect sunlight and turn it into electric power

In 1986, the Soviet Union launched a space station, called *Mir*, into orbit. Astronauts are able to live and work on board *Mir* for months at a time. Unmanned spacecraft from Earth bring them fresh supplies of food and equipment.

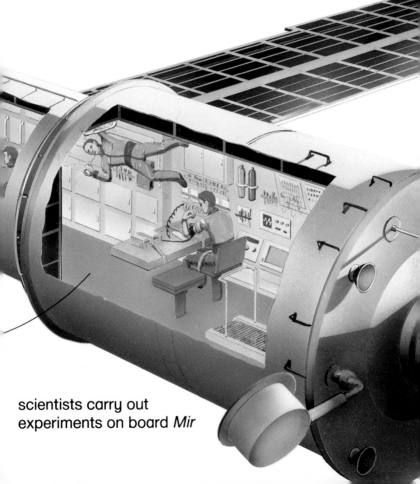

scientists carry out experiments on board *Mir*

Giant telescopes

Astronomers use powerful telescopes here on Earth and in Space to see far across the Universe.

This giant telescope sits on Palomar Mountain in California nearly 2,000 metres up. Here the air is especially clear and the weather is almost always good.

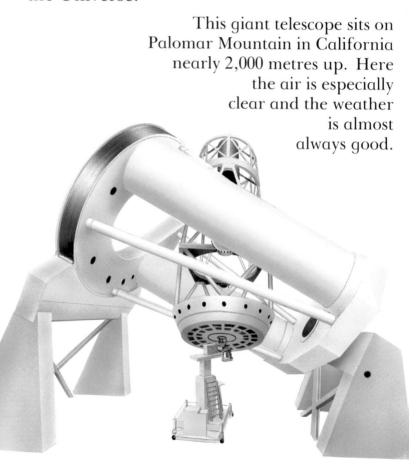

The Hubble Telescope is the biggest telescope in Space. It can see a lot more than ground telescopes because it is above the blanket of air that surrounds the Earth.

Hubble can see millions of distant galaxies.

Radio telescopes

As well as giving off light, many stars and galaxies give off powerful radio signals. Astronomers can pick up these radio signals using radio telescopes.

These smaller radio telescopes can turn to listen to any part of the sky. Astronomers link several of them together in a chain to get a stronger signal.

This giant radio telescope in France is more than 200 metres long and 35 metres high. Because it is fixed in one position, it can only pick up signals from stars that pass directly in front of it as the Earth turns.

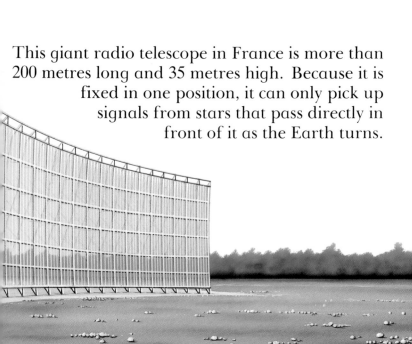

⊷ Earth calling Space

The biggest radio telescope in the world is at Arecibo in Puerto Rico. It is 305 metres wide and fills the entire crater of an old volcano. It can't move by itself, but as the Earth turns, it slowly scans the sky for radio signals.

In 1974, Arecibo was used to send a radio message to a cluster of stars in the constellation of Hercules. The message will take 25,000 years to get to its destination. Scientists hope there may be other living beings in Space who might hear it one day.

The Arecibo message was made up of 1,679 tiny characters. They form a code that other intelligent beings should be able to understand.

At home in Space

The idea of living in Space may seem impossible, but already engineers and scientists are planning a base on the Moon. People could be living and working there by the year 2050.

This first lunar base will probably be a mining camp. Astronauts have found that Moon rocks contain metals such as aluminium and titanium. These could be mined and brought back to Earth.

Amazing facts

The first living thing from Earth ever to travel in Space was a little Russian dog called Laika, in November 1957.

The first man in Space was Yuri Gagarin of the Soviet Union. On 12 April, 1961, he circled the Earth once in his spacecraft *Vostok 1*. His trip lasted 108 minutes.

Pioneer 10 was the first space probe to leave the solar system. It carries a picture of the Sun and its nine planets, as well as a picture of a man and a woman in case other intelligent beings ever find it.

The footprints of the astronauts who landed on the Moon will last for millions of years. This is because there is no wind or rain on the Moon to disturb them.

Deep in

Space

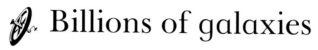 Billions of galaxies

Our galaxy, the Milky Way, is just one of billions of other galaxies in the Universe. Galaxies come in many shapes and sizes.

Spiral galaxies have two arms that slowly revolve round a central ball of stars.

In a barred spiral galaxy the arms revolve round a central bar of stars.

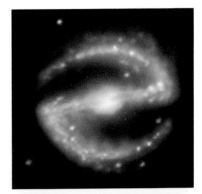

Some galaxies are simply great balls of stars. These are called elliptical galaxies. Usually, they are made up of very old stars.

Certain galaxies don't seem to have any shape at all. They are called irregular galaxies.

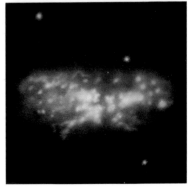

Accidents in Space

Even though the distance between the galaxies is huge, sometimes two galaxies collide with each other. These collisions take place over millions of years, but astronomers can use computers to work out what happens.

1. Two galaxies draw near to each other.

2. Their outer stars start to mix.

3. The cores of the two galaxies come together.

4. The two cores drift apart again.

5. What is left are two swirls of stars with completely new shapes.

116

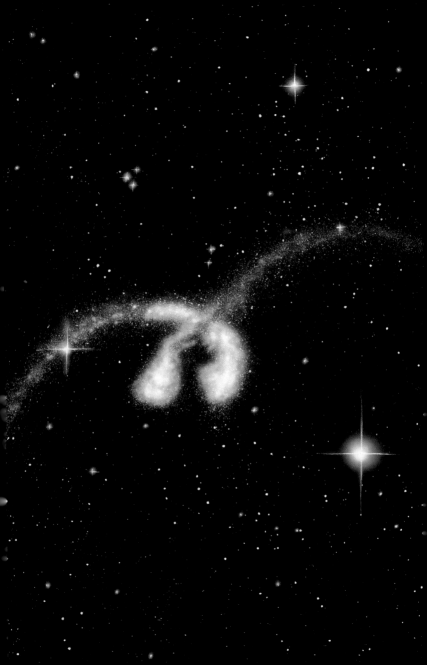

A big mystery

Scientists are fairly sure that the Universe began with a huge explosion called the 'Big Bang'. They also believe that the Universe is getting bigger as the galaxies move farther and farther apart. Perhaps the Universe will just keep on growing for ever. Or perhaps one day the galaxies will start moving back together again and the Universe will end in a 'Big Crunch'. Nobody knows.

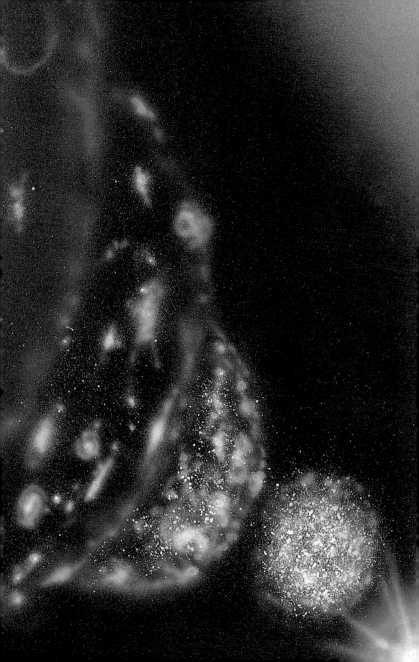

Amazing facts

Galaxies exist in groups. Our galaxy, the Milky Way, is part of a group of about 30 galaxies called the Local Group.

Our closest neighbours in the Local Group are two galaxies called the Large Magellanic Cloud and the Small Magellanic Cloud. People living in the southern half of the Earth can see both galaxies as hazy patches of light in the night sky.

Scientists believe that, as well as all the planets, galaxies and stars that we can see, the Universe contains a lot of dark material that is completely invisible.

INDEX